BareBackMagazine

June 2014

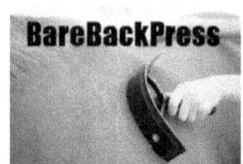

BareBackPress
Hamilton, Ontario, Canada
For enquires visit www.barebackpress.com
For information contact press@barebacklit.com

Editors Mike Algera and Peter Jelen
Cover layout and art: "The Retro Social Network" © 2014 Peter Jelen.

POETRY

FICTION

POETRY

lotus blossoms in the spring
Carl Miller Daniels

bradley was driving.
matthew was sitting in the seat beside him.
every time the car hit a pothole,
matthew spurted
out a little teeny-tiny bit of cum.
whenever they hit a pothole, and matthew spurted out a little
teeny-tiny bit of cum, bradley laughed.
bradley was
sexy, fully
dressed, driving
in his usual manner, which
 was kind of fast,
and reasonably
cautious.
matthew was sexy, outrageously
 handsome, and totally
naked. matthew had a big
smooth hard-on.
the car hit another
pothole.
matthew spurted out a little
 teeny-tiny bit of cum.
bradley laughed, and pushed the accelerator
a little further toward the floor.
then bradley said: "hey, matthew, does it feel
good everytime you spurt a little bit of cum? does
it feel
like a real orgasm?"
matthew, sitting there sexy naked and
big-dicked hard as a rock, said, "almost.
though it doesn't last as long as a regular orgasm,
of course. this one is just really really fast,
but real nice, too."
bradley purposefully steered the car
over a pothole. matthew spurted out
another teeny-tiny little bit of cum.
bradley laughed.
matthew blotted his own flat naked sexy belly

with a wadded up kleenex, and then tossed
it into the back of the car.
"and what kind of drug did you say you took
to get this reaction?" asked Bradley,
guiding the car smoothly and carefully
through traffic.
"don't know," said matthew. "the guy
didn't tell me.
he just told me
what it'd do. so i thought,
what the heck... give it
a try..."
bradley, fully clothed,
driving the car, said,
"you total goof!"
"pretty much," said matthew.
matthew, totally naked, big smooth dick
nice and
 hard, smiled coquettishly.
bradley hit another pothole.
matthew spurted out another teeny-tiny bit of
cum.
both guys laughed like maniacs.
it was exactly that kind of day.

jeans and a t-shirt
Carl Miller Daniels

as the words poured out of his mouth like
droplets of cum spurting out of his dick,
the sexy naked young man
told the guy who was jerking him off,
"god oh god that feels great i'm cumming
i'm cumming i'm spurting i'm hard
as a rock and i'm spurting cum and
spurting cum and spurting
more cum and spurting cum
feels incredibly incredibly goooood. god."
**

"my turn," says the guy who just
jerked off the first guy.
**

now, the guy who is getting jerked
off by the first guy, the talkative
guy, is the quiet type.
he just stands there while
the
 talkative guy
 jerks him
off from behind.
they both watch the whole procedure
in the big
 mirror on the back
of the bedroom door.
**

silent guy spurts cum.
silent guy spurts a LOT of cum.
**

after silent guy
spurts cum, talkative guy starts
talking again, and says, "i still
don't know why you don't want
me to say anything while i'm
jerking YOU off, especially
since you never say anything
yourself. don't you want

to talk about it? don't you
want to talk about how
incredibly good it feels
getting jerked off and
spurting cum?"
**

silent guy turns around
and looks at talkative guy.
silent guy says, "i like
my coffee black. you like
yours with lots of cream and
sugar. get it?"
**

talkative guy nods,
smiles. once again,
they are happy
in their relationship,
secure in their love.

About the Author:
Carl Miller Daniels lives in the United States. He's not a cowboy, but thinks about
them a lot. His poems have appeared in many nice places, including Assaracus,
BareBack Magazine, Chiron Review, Citizens for Decent Literature, The
Commonline Journal, DNA Magazine, My Favorite Bullet, and Zygote in my
Coffee. Daniels has three chapbooks in print. And his first full-length book, Gorilla
Architecture, was recently published by Interior Noise Press. His next full-length
book, Saline, is in the works, also at Interior Noise Press. Daniels and his partner,
Jon (aka "the sweetest man in the world"), have lived together for over 30 years.

Vaseline
Wayne F. Burke

It was after the abortion:
her suggestion:
I said "go get it"
and she got out of bed
and her feet
pat pat pat
to the bathroom and back
and I took the jar from her hand
and spread some goo on her
as she waited, on all fours
patient as a dog
and then I got behind her
and I slid it in
past the sphincter
and into air:
like fucking a balloon
but she liked it
maybe because
it was how her mother took it
once a month
from the old man
who beat her first
and always said
afterward
"she's got an ass that just won't quit."

Stabbed
Wayne F. Burke

I told her while we were
lying in bed:
told her it was over.
She started to weep and
I wanted to comfort her
but could not...would not
and got up and went out
to the kitchen
and poured myself a drink
and she came out of the room
a little later
dry-eyed
and without any clothes on
but not really naked
and said "if I had a knife
when you told me
I'd of stabbed you"
and how glad I was
then
that I had told her in bed
and not in a restaurant.

About the Author:
Wayne F. Burke's poetry has appeared or is forthcoming in Bluestem, Red Savina, Black Wire, Forge, Sassafras, Dead Flowers, The Packingtown Review, Crack of the Spine, Bottle Rockets, and elsewhere. His book of poems WORDS THAT BURN is published by Bareback Press (2013). He lives in the central Vermont area.

Protection Racket
Till Gwinn

All the hustle of Manhattan fan belts and napalm hum
sticks to my senses;
eyes filled by fire, mouth mustard gas, ears drone bombs
with engendering sobs of
holy mobs.

They say it's for protection,
for insurance, security:
pride.
But I find all the best cacophony
exposes right outliers
to be superseded by the mean,
without clout accusations of treason,
just lovers' language: drastic, growing like the
Horn of Plenty
into the
Skull of Power.

About the Author:
Till Gwinn is a 23 year-old poet/landscaper from Oregon City, OR.

The Magic Leper
Stephen Philip Druce

"I thought I was ugly until I saw him"
she said, pointing to the crowded café he was sitting in.

But this soul of lonely candle wick,
with a face like melted wax,
performed for them a card trick -
turning aces into jacks.

With the speed of a downhill car chase,
with a rolling of the drums,
he juggled knives and forks with grace
and turned them into sticky buns.

So now they couldn't take their eyes off him,
his hands as quick as tiger paws,
he stood and took a bow with a grin
to spontaneous applause.
They yelled "more! more!"
so for an encore -
white doves flew from inside his tea-pot
he`d sprinkled with salt and pepper,
with tears he cried "pretty I`m not, but I am the magic leper!"

About the Author:

Stephen Philip Druce is a forty nine year old music teacher from Shrewsbury (birthplace of Charles Darwin), in the UK. In his college days, his literature tutors nicknamed him 'The Real Fantasist' - referring to the vivid imagination he displayed in his fiction based essays. Stephen's poetry is published in UK magazines - Fade Poetry, The Screeching Owl, and Pulsar Magazine. He enjoys reading WH Auden, Charles Bukowski, Philip Larkin, Dylan Thomas and John Keats.

I'D LIKE TO TEACH THE WORLD TO SING
Kenneth Pobo

In the early 70s we tried to buy
the world a Coke. The world said no
to our carbonation. How sad
to stand on a hilltop in Italy,
the world looking the other way.

It's still looking the other way,
yet we follow after,
only to see it making love
to two strangers in a park.

We should turn away,
sip our Coke and get to urgent tasks.

Instead, we watch.

We wish we were the world.

Or one of the strangers.

STOP THE WORLD
Kenneth Pobo

The first gay song
I heard on the radio,
Flamin' Ember's
"Stop The World
(And Let Me Off),"

February 1971. The singer,
upset because he loved a woman
who loved a woman,
wanted to leave
the world.

This theatrical response
seems silly now,
but then, I thought wow,
someone is actually singing
about a gay situation
despite the endlessly
crashing waves of hetero-
sexual love songs.

A high school junior,
I knew I was gay.
Religion kept
patting my fanny.

It took a while to tell it
to keep its hands
to itself. Other hands
gave me a hand.

The world didn't stop.

About the Author:
Kenneth Pobo had a chapbook published in 2013 by Eastern Point Press called
Placemats. His work has appeared in: Grain, Mudfish, The Fiddlehead, Hawaii
Review, and elsewhere. Follow him at @KenPobo on Twitter.

Hands Holding the Void (Invisible Object)
(after the sculpture by Alberto Giacometti)
Neil Ellman

Whether a wish or a loss
an empty jar or invisible harp
held like a crying child
as if it would fall and break
into a hundred forgotten parts
it is everything we cannot see
or feel, remember how
our fingers touched the shape
of its reality before it was even born
in the cup of our hands
and suddenly disappeared
behind our eyes
a thing without a name.

Woman with Her Throat Cut
(after the sculpture by Alberto Giacometti)
Neil Ellman

The police report that hers was a little death,
a petite morph , as the French would say,
like the others who died in the throes of embrace
or at the hands of a stranger she chose;
little, too, by her insignificance, not worth
another moment of their time.

She was found in an alleyway
feet from the many passersby
who walk the streets without a second glance
unrecognizable, half-eaten by rats
and the ravages of a tortured life,
battered, wounded, raped,
reduced to this crustacean form
a victim of misogyny
less than human
less than woman
less alive.

About the Author:
Neil Ellman, a poet from New Jersey, has been nominated for the Pushcart Prize, Best of the Net and Rhysling Award. More than 950 of his poems, many of which are ekphrastic and written in response to works of modern and contemporary art, appear in print and online journals, anthologies and chapbooks throughout the world.

Why I'm not a Numbers Kinda Guy
Mike Algera

They wear grey blouses and slacks,
hair tied in
buns and buzz cuts and
horn rimmed glasses --
they deal in suitcases, spreadsheets
and equations.
Brackets are brackish.
Code doesn't compliment cursive.

Being 27 doesn't give me vitality --
only words can spell out
my sentence, the semblance and
sublime of word
pictures scratch the dotted
line of existence --
me, I find solace in a calculator
with a dirty mind

some say it's wisdom
some say it's sadism
to read too deep into

5318008

when turned upside
down.
The word has been translated
into dozens of languages,

but it's not flattering
dialogue to an accountant
or a waitress
when the check slips
past your meal
like anthrax, especially when you
recall ordering
dessert ---
and that's when
you need
a drink.

Patience, Outburst, Daydream
or
my brother's mood swings in threes
Mike Algera

I.

Whenever my dad decides
to take a YouTube day
my brother gnashes his teeth --
pulverizing the enamel
into grains
you could collect
in a salt shaker

"I'll never forgive you,"
he says, "For showing him
how to use YouTube!"
I'm starting to miss
the Moody Blues greatest hits CD.
My dad watches Westerns
for free, my brother is afraid
of the dentist, and my salt
shaker collection
is
growing.

II.

"More butt-fucking cowboys! Fuck
Saturdays and AMC!"
My dad watches cowboy films
on Saturdays, calls them
Pioneer stories.
My brother needs six cups of coffee
for fuel, electrocution
of the nerves, plucking
of violin strings.
"Calling the cowboy a 'cowboy' is
considered derogatory," he says.
My brother, gnashing his teeth

calls my dad
everything but
cowboy or
pioneer
whenever he's outside
sucking
down cigarettes and booze
on his imaginary ranch
imagining the car as his horse,
saloon and bedroom.
"The Pioneers left legacies
not legends."
My brother pumps more electricity
into his body.
His teeth have yellowed
a shade of brown.
I'm not a violinist
I'm a collector of salt shakers

III.

My dad is sleeping
on the couch, using
my mom's pillow
snoring, drooling
dreaming of the Pioneer days,
pressing his ear
to my mom's pillow, toward
earth's incubating engine,
the majestic herd of buffalo
taking the helm of his dreamscape –
my brother walks into the room
where my dad sleeps
sharpening his tongue.
His teeth now rusty nails
gnawing into my dad's throat,
the snoring sputters, the
drooling spurts,
my mom's pillow permanently
indented

my brother's teeth yellowed
another shade of brown.
He has no use for dentistry
and my salt shaker collection
is
growing.

About the Author:
Mike Algera's first full length poetry book, Old Gods for New is now available in
print and as an e-book at www.BareBackPress.com. He has been published by Arc
Poetry Magazine, BareBack Lit, Hamilton Arts & Letters, Nostrovia Poetry and
Cyclamens & Swords Publishing. His favourite themes include dysfunctional
families, Oriental mysticism, vigilante justice, love and love in all of the wrong
places. He lives in Hamilton Ontario, with his high maintenance dog, Grendel.
His home away from home is in digital la-la land, at www.mikealgera.com.

True religion
Dave Migman

Walk the street, cock-sure and fuck-pure
hands vibrating in your pocket gloves
hoods shaking in your presence
young doe with a mouthful of cum.
See, it's easy like that. It's easy.
On their knees before you – each and every one
kind of a fixation with you
like groping the ball bag security
while the eyes swell and saliva flows

We ruck amongst the clicking machines
whirring fans, circuit board precision
We grunt on the ground like hogs at the trough
surrendering to primal necessity
Tower blocks surround us, we fuck on buses,
in turbo motors behind the console our juice
oils the machine, we primitives,
we animals, sexing, licking, stroking,
playing, pruning, raping, fucking, fucking
in the shadow of our technology, our science,
our religion

About the Author:
Dave Migman is a writer, artist and stone carver from the UK. His novel The Wolf
Stepped Out is available from Doghorn Publishing. He has spoken word albums
available from Splitting Sounds Records and links via his Soundcloud Page
(http://soundcloud.com/dave-migman).

How the Game Works
William Doreski

Scripting major league baseball
requires massaging the rules
and complete disdain for the fans.
They pay me ten dollars a game
to renumber the bases, corrupt
the umpires, choreograph
run-downs, write lead into bats
and spittle into pitches. I choose
winners and losers according
to mood and the bets I place
with the sleaziest bookies I know.
Everyone knows the games are rigged
but few know who delivers
the scripts later discovered
by reporters prowling clubhouses
after the players head for the bars.
Because I despise home-town crowds
I favor visiting teams
by devising lurid plays
featuring ghastly errors
like balls thrown into the stands
and bobbles of easy pop flies
that make the locals groan and curse.
For a lousy ten dollars a game
I'm not about to crown another
Babe Ruth, Lou Gehrig, or Cy Young.
No one's stats will look impressive
when the current season collapses
in a World Series comedy
of passed balls, struck batters, strikeouts
and winning runs walked home. Too bad
baseball isn't life, but what,
then, is? Averaging fifteen games
per day I make a bare living;
but sometimes when I see players
on TV pull pages of script
from their pockets and shake their heads
in disbelief I'm so proud

I could cry aloft to the heavens
that I'm keeping American strong.

About the Author:
William Doreski lives in Peterborough, New Hampshire, and teaches at Keene State College. His most recent book of poetry is The Suburbs of Atlantis (2013). He has published three critical studies, including Robert Lowell's Shifting Colors. His essays, poetry, fiction, and reviews have appeared in many journals.

Plead
Devona Brown

Please, please, please be aware of this: it's not a continual thing, you must understand. It's gradual, like ink sliding up—no down—after tipping over on the table. Of course, the mahogany wood stains black as the river of unformed words dribbles to the edge. Drip. Drip. Dark rain lands on the faded and yellow linoleum floor; leaving splotches of brown stains; insects puddled onto speeding car windows. Such wastes of energy.

About the Author:
Devo Brown is a writer whose work has appeared in Hamline's Women Studies newsletter, The Fulcrum and The Paper Lantern. She works part time as a Communications Intern for Westminster Presbyterian Church in Minneapolis while finishing her BFA in Creative Writing. She lives in St. Louis Park with her daughter and two cats.

The High Priestess/La Papesse (2)
Caitlin Johnson

What I love is--
well, no one gives a shit what I love.
I am a dead woman
to them, one set aside like Mary
in a crèche, here only to serve
the whims of their god.

I heard them whispering once
from beyond the altar:
She speaks to God and I can't
even remember his name.
If I told them it was a sham,
they would wonder at this blessing
handed down to me, how I dare
to spit on it, my unholy vitriol
spewing forth.

Fuck it. If they want to converse
with their absent god, let
them try it. Once.

About the Author:
Caitlin Johnson is the Managing Editor of CAIRN: The St. Andrews Review. She holds a Master of Fine Arts in Creative Writing from Lesley University. Her work has appeared in All Things Girl, Black Mirror Magazine, Charlotte Viewpoint, Fortunates, Pembroke Magazine, Vagina: The Zine, and What the Fiction, among other outlets.

FICTION

The Worth of Love Letters
J.J. Steinfeld

Randall liked riding the bus, especially on Saturdays. In fact, bus-riding was not only a form of recreation for him, it provided him the opportunity to write. He even considered a bus to be somewhat of an office. This Saturday, which seemed extra special to him because it was exactly a year since his heart attack and he was feeling better than ever, Randall sat next to a window and wrote sentence after sentence on the new pad of yellow legal paper he had bought that morning. When he reached the bottom of a page, he flipped the sheet over and began on the next. He always wrote longhand on yellow legal paper, as if he were incapable of being creative unless it was on this type of paper, and on a moving bus. Maybe, he had considered on several occasions, he was incapable of writing anywhere except on a bus. He attempted to write on other types of paper and in other places, but he could never sustain any sort of creative thought outside his moving-through-the-city writing office. These thoughts were soon cast aside by the surge of creativity he was experiencing, the beautiful love letter he was writing, to Theda Bara, whose picture he had found on the internet. He had been quite taken with her, even though he had never seen one of her films. Earlier he had attempted to write letters to other long-ago film stars, Mary Pickford and Mae West, but both of those letters had faltered. Theda Bara had stirred something within him. This was the hundredth love letter he had written on a bus and he intended to put them together in a collection to submit for publication. He had already chosen a title: *The Love Letters of a Broken-hearted Bus Rider.*

Now the words were flowing and he stopped only occasionally to look out the window at the city passing by. He tried to imagine the love letters the people he saw would write. He imagined letters that were sweet and almost innocent; others that were lascivious verbal romps. And, he thought, every emotion and desire from one end to the other of the love-letter spectrum. Randall felt good as the ride continued.

At first Randall didn't sense the woman who sat down next to him. In an aisle seat, she read a magazine, glancing once in a while at Randall as he wrote. When he paused from his intense, almost frenetic writing and looked down at the floor of the bus, he first noticed the woman, or rather her shoes. They were open-toed sandals and her nails were painted bright red. He thought of the colour as blood red, and then cringed, not liking the connotations. He turned to look at her, as if a magician had made her magically appear out of nowhere. She was perhaps nine or ten years younger than he, that was his guess, and she was reading an issue of a magazine that he had seen the cover of at the convenience store where he had purchased his legal pad. He also remembered thinking that the person on the cover of the magazine had an unkind, severe face and would have written the most inept, unloving love letters, if he had ever been in love.

As Randall was looking out the window, the woman said, "I've never seen anyone write so fast."

Randall smiled and said, "The words rarely flow this quickly for me, but my creative juices are bubbling deliciously this afternoon."

"Deliciously, indeed," the woman said and smiled. Randall started to compose a love letter to her in his head. He was leaning more toward the sweet and innocent, when she said, "I'm amazed you can write so well on a bus."

"Not always. Creative juices aside, everything seems to have come together today."

"What you writing there?" the woman asked, squinting at Randall's legal pad, and Randall, making no effort to hide his words, said, "Love letters."

"You must be in love big time," she said, arching her eyebrows ever so slightly.

"No, not presently. But I like writing about love...love letters. You might call it a literary hobby."

"You have an unusual hobby."

"Bit of an obsession of mine."

"How can you have a bit of an obsession? Obsessions are obsessions."

"You have an excellent point, I admit. Do you have any old love letters lying around?"

"I wouldn't show them to anyone."

"They have a life of their own if someone else reads them. The love continues, so to speak." He looked at her feet again, the bright-red toenails, and he noticed for the first time that each of the little toes were not painted, as if she had run out of polish. How could he have missed that before? He began to alter the direction of the mental love letter. It became more about the physical and desire, almost erotic.

"There are as many good memories as bad memories in my love letters," the woman said, closing her magazine.

"I think I understand what you mean. My grandfather on my mother's side proposed to my grandmother in 1931 while they were dancing to the song 'Love Letters in the Sand.' I adored that story, all the different versions that my grandparents used to tell when I was a kid."

"That qualifies as a good memory of love."

"The connection gets more incredible and loving. My parents told me they were necking in a car and listening to 'Love Letters in the Sand,' the 1957 version, sung by Pat Boone. My mother is still alive, but my father died a few years ago."

"That's lovely synchronicity, isn't it?"

"I'm divorced now, but when I proposed to the then love of my life, it was at a beach and I wrote the words 'Will you marry me?' in the sand, and whistled 'Love Letters in the Sand' as I was doing it and waiting for her reply."

"I've been married twice—and twice divorced. Probably didn't have the right love song to help me through either marriage."

"Despite your marriages ending, I'm sure you've received love letters in your life."

"Nothing all that memorable."

Randall liked to tell people he had the world's largest collection of love letters. He put ads on the internet offering to purchase any particularly passionate love letters people might have in their possession. Of course, most of the letters he was offered weren't authentic, but that didn't matter to him. They were genuine love letters if someone, for whatever reason, claimed they were. He used them to help with the writing of love letters for the book he was working on. All of a sudden he changed the working title of the book to *The Imaginary Love Letters of an Unimaginable Bus Rider*. He caught himself being a little too explicit in his letter, the lustful overtaking the affectionate, and crossed out several words.

"A well-written love letter is a joy to read. Furthermore, even a poorly written love letter by someone famous or villainous, let's say, has an intrinsic worth."

The woman stared at him without saying anything and he felt she was questioning his thinking. "The villainous can write love letters, can't they?" he said.

"I'm certain they can," the woman said and absently flipped the pages of the magazine on her lap.

"What I wouldn't give for a love letter by Mata Hari," Randall said, resisting an impulse to stop the woman from flipping the pages of her magazine. He said it would be priceless and the woman sitting next to him said everything in the world had a price. No, Randall argued, some things were priceless, had to be priceless, or else why was life worth living. The woman said that was an idiotic argument. Randall thought briefly about moving to another seat, but he noticed that the bus was now full. The woman said she looked upon his obsession with love letters, the love letters of others, as compensation for something lacking in his life. Randall said that nothing was lacking in his life, each day was a gift, not only because it had been exactly a year since his heart attack and he was feeling energetic and amorous, but because it was his intention, his plan, his destiny, to be the recipient of the most love letters, after writing the most passionate, interesting love letter ever. "According to who?" the woman asked. "According to whom," Randall said, and began to laugh more vigorously than he ever remembered laughing. The woman shook her head at Randall's laughing, saying love makes a person silly, but she had never realised the thought of love letters would bring on such silliness. Randall stood up from his seat, still laughing, and got off at the wrong bus stop.

About the Author:
Fiction writer, poet, and playwright J. J. Steinfeld lives on Prince Edward Island, where he is patiently waiting for Godot's arrival and a phone call from Kafka. While waiting, he has published fourteen books, including Should the Word Hell Be Capitalized? (Stories, Gaspereau Press), Anton Chekhov Was Never in Charlottetown (Stories, Gaspereau Press), Would You Hide Me? (Stories, Gaspereau Press), An Affection for Precipices (Poetry, Serengeti Press), Misshapenness (Poetry, Ekstasis Editions), and A Glass Shard and Memory (Stories, Recliner Books).

Misogyny is Best Served Hot in Stella's Milano
Joseph Cruse

"Fucking old bitches, man."

During the summer, I started working in what was considered an upscale, Midwestern, Italian restaurant to pay for my rent and other basic survival needs. The food was tasty, but, a week after I started slinging plates to patrons, the chicken breasts only hung low and heavy and the fettuccine alfredo was simply noodles and an off-grey liquid semen.

But I needed the money, and like the best of whores I know how to keep my mouth shut.

The restaurant was a prison, complete with standard black garb and little to no appreciation for the menial tasks that serving requires.

Learn the routine and the business might not swallow your soul.

Smile. Wash your hands. Set up tables with coffee plates and silverware – two forks and one knife. Stand around for twenty minutes while no one comes in. Smile. Greet the patron and seat them at the appropriate table. Offer alcohol (because 1) someone may as well have it since you aren't and 2) it costs more and will effectively get you a bigger tip) or other beverages. Smile. Say specials.

"You hear me? Fucking old bitches, man."

Ask for appetizers. Take entrée order. Bring out bread (two per person plus two for the table) and salads made of two types of lettuce, cheeses, and secret dressing. Always ask how the food is. Smile. Bring out entrées. Smile. Ask how the food is. Take away plates. Check for coffee (Starbucks regular) or dessert (look at the fucking menu). Smile. Drop check. Take check. Check tab to see if you were paid well, you weren't. Watch last table leave. Do side work. Take money. Go home. Sleep. Wake up. Smile. Repeat.

After working at Stella for sixth months, I had an overdeveloped alcohol tolerance and was strongly considering hard drugs. Most of my serving cohorts had been at the routine since the restaurant opened six years ago. They also had overdeveloped tolerances for alcohol and hard drugs – which was why most of them were working in a restaurant in the first place.

"Yes. I hear you. Old bitches. Jesus, they're always out there. They don't tip well and we still have to serve them. Such is life."

"Eight fucking dollars off a seven top. They each want water, decaf, and separate checks, and then sit around for three fucking hours and order salads. I can't stand bitches man. I hope their walkers bend and their shuttle bus veers into a ditch. It's no different, man. All these women are a bunch of crazy bitches. Come in here order salads and water. God, I wish. I just wish once a month I could walk up and punch one of these women in the face. You know? Have a freebee? Just walk up and BAM. Punch a bitch in the face."

"I would suggest not doing that. It reflects badly upon your character."

"I wouldn't fuck one girl who worked here. Except one, right? You know, and she can't fucking stand me."

"No shit. But you ever asked her why?"

"Hell no, unless I'm inside her what do I care?"

"That's why you're alone and probably have some deep-seated homosexual proclivity that you're repressing and that, hopefully, drives you insane later in life. I've got to put this order in, leave me the fuck alone so I can think for a second."

"That's alright, brother, got to take more water to these fucking old ladies anyway."

Smile.

II.

Every day I work with Seth I get slapped on the ass. Not in a borderline flirtatious-heterosexual-dominant way that most married men slap other men, but more like a wound up- windmill slap that echoes throughout the restaurant and stings like a motherfucker.

"Goddammit, Seth."

"I want you to be inside me." He whispers in my ear.

"Seth, for the last time I won't do that to your wife. You're a freak. Fuck off."

He looked hurt.

"You really think I'm a freak?"

"No. You're just you being you. You may be a bit of a freak, but I try to accept people for who they are."

"What do you mean? What type of person are you saying I am?

"You're like a big great dane that doesn't know the size of his body. You have lots of love to give, but your hips and head are too big to not break everything around you. Loving intention, but poor execution. Don't ever fucking slap me again."

"Do you think I'm crazy?"

"Yes, but I don't like you as a person."

III.

Elvis was the only black man that got to cook food, but only on mornings – the other three scrubbed the dishes. On a wait staff of 54, there were only 4 black men on the entire roster, and no more than two were ever in the kitchen at the same time.

Seth and Elvis were talking, as per usual, behind the line before any customers had arrived.

"Motherfucker, yes, I have your Pasta-9-Tails. It'll be a minute motherfucker. Get the fuck outta here."

"Elvis, I'm hungry man. Hurry, people are gonna be here. You know you only give me shit because I married the bigass white woman you wanted."

"Hey listen, want? Motherfucker, back when your girl worked on the line it was just all night long. 'Oh Elvis, please cut those carrots for me.' 'Oh Elvis, would you plate up those potatoes for me.' 'Oh Elvis, sauté that fucking broccoli.' 'Oh Elvis...' All night long motherfucker.

The grill cook next to Elvis laughed.

Seth smiled. "Elvis that has to be unsanitary."

"It wasn't unsanitary, motherfucker. We cleaned up after. Then you go along and steal the bitch away. Why you gotta go around and be fucking up a good thing?"

"Just finish my goddamn pasta, Elvis."

Seth started to cut bread at a sharp angle, and the knife grated against the crust of the bread shredding its soft insides.

"What are you staring at motherfucker? Don't you have a table or nothing?"

Elvis caught me staring as the whole scene unfolded.

"Sorry Elvis, I've been waiting for my food for twenty minutes while you've been talking."

"Motherfucker, your shit's almost up."

That meant I would be waiting at least another five minutes while my table sat outside wondering why it took longer than ten minutes to make two orders of glorified spaghetti-o's.

"Dammit, Elvis."

He threw up two ceramic plates and went back to his line. I went up to grab my food.

"That ain't yours. Hey Seth, you up, motherfucker."

IV.

The restaurant is a trap. It is one of the only places that actively encourages its workers to be lazy while demanding that they be constantly doing something for the benefit of the restaurant.

The opening manager Sean was a skinny, goateed, ball-buster who had penchant for multicolored clothing. His hair was always gelled, his shoes were always shined, and his shirts were regularly ironed. I'm pretty sure the man only owned pink or purple button downs and paisley ties.

"You know, at Stella one of our top priorities is the appearance of things, right?"

The other week he made me re-vacuum the entire floor because he found seven bread crumbs next to the table and one morning he felt it necessary to teach me how to sweep – "No, you use two hands and sweep back and forth in a wide arc. Have you ever used a broom before?" His obsession with cleanliness was an outlet to demonstrate his power over those that had the misfortune to fail his expectations.

"What's wrong with the way I look?"

He looked me up and down, analyzing how I failed at each point of the workplace garb.

"Your shoes are dirty."

"They're covered in spaghetti sauce, bread crumbs, and butter. You can't keep shoes clean in this place. What do you expect?"

"Your pants have too much lint on them."

"I've already lint rolled my pants twice now. I'm not going to do it again."

"Your tie isn't straight."

"Yeah, but I still have to fix that."

"Your apron is dirty."

"You got me there boss."

There were alfredo and meat sauce stains all along the sides of my apron. I only wipe it down with a wet rag before my shift. I wasn't going to wash an apron each night just to get it dirty the next day.

"Do you even own a comb?"

"I haven't combed my hair in two years. Towel and fingers."

"Jesus. How do you even exist?"

"I scrape by with a charming smile."

I smiled.

"Just go and put the fucking silverware down."

"It's your world, boss man."

He turned and saw the hostess wiping down the walls.

"For fuck's sake. Does no one do anything around here? When you wipe down the walls you go from the top to the bottom. Wax on, wax off. How hard is that? Just fucking stupid. When you're done with that, come find me and I'll show you how to do the rest of your damn job."

I walked over to Laurel. "At least you're pretty. He can't give you shit for that."

"No, how I looked was his problem last week. Why do you think we can't wear spaghetti straps anymore?

"He shouldn't talk to you like a dick."

"I've worked here for three years. He talks that way to me all the time."

"I know. Doesn't mean he isn't an ass."

"What can you do? It's Stella."

Laurel went back to the walls, and I went back to the forks. The restaurant was about to open.

About the Author:
Joseph Cruse is an English Master's student at the University of Illinois - Springfield. Recently transplanted to Louisiana, he continues to write, act, spray graffiti scenes of movies onto canvas, tutor, and, more often than not, get into some trouble. He has also been published in Poetry Quarterly and CACTI Magazine.

Beauty
Cody T. Luff

His name was Beauty but he wasn't. Her hair was wet with his sweat, his face a glowing cigarette in the darkness. She did not love him tonight.

"Twenty," he said. His legs moved against the hotel chair. He smoked.

Beauty had answered her question and she brought her knees against her slick belly. It was good he wasn't on the bed.

"So many." She smelled him, smelled herself, even in the reek of his cigarette. He had fucked her for what seemed like hours before he finally came.

"Yeah. Guess so."

She could make out his knuckles, the cigarette jutting between. She hated that he smoked but liked the way his hands moved when he did.

Beauty finished his cigarette and reached for another, his face coming into the light from the window. At one time he had looked like a boy, had looked like so many other boys to her. In this light he looked like something else, something sexless and old.

This was Beauty's room. The one he liked. It was twenty bucks a night but it was the first room he fucked her in. He said there was something about the room that got him hard.

She thought about dressing, wondered how Beauty would take it if she put something on. You didn't do things before Beauty wanted them done.

"What's with the bruise?" Beauty said behind his cigarette.

She looked down at her arms, the light was dim but she knew what Beauty was looking at.

"Nothing," she said, drawing her arms against her chest.

"Somebody do that?" Beauty said. His voice was soft and she closed her eyes against it.

"No."

"You spike?" His voice was softer, the cigarette no longer against his lips.

"No." It was true. There'd been a needle but it wasn't something going into her veins. It had been going out.

"You going to tell me?" It sounded like a question. It wasn't.

"Doctor." She moved up the bed, against the current of sheets and pillows, she put her nude back against the low headboard.

"You went to the doctor?" The cigarette moved back to his lips.

"Yeah."

"What, are you sick?" Beauty had a low voice and it could be chocolate and rum, it could unzip, unlace and slip off and bring slickness to things. But it was always that way and he wasn't always interested in what was under her clothes.

"Yeah." She placed a pillow over her stomach, leaning over it, letting her hair fall over her face, hiding him from her.

Beauty smoked, his free hand trailing down to his prick. Beauty wasn't big, not anywhere but inside his skull. Sometimes that made her love him.

"What's wrong with you?" He crushed his cigarette out, rattling the little plastic ash tray.

She moved then, pushing her pillow away, sliding on her knees the length of the bed, showing him everything she knew he wanted. His body responded to her, but Beauty and Beauty's body were two different men.

"What's wrong with you?" he said again.

"Come on..." she said; she slipped off the bed, her hands finding his cock.

He leaned forward, his face in the light. His hands, cold and soft, touched her face smelling of nicotine. "What's wrong?"

She wished she were back on the bed.

"Tell me," Beauty said. His face close to hers. He'd never hit her. Not that she was unfamiliar with being hit. Everybody got theirs sometime. You just had to decide whether to hit back. She knew she'd never hit Beauty back. Nobody did, unless they wanted to be twenty one. Somebody had to be twenty one.

"I...I was pregnant."

Beauty looked into her eyes and she waited, her hand still on his cock. He leaned back, rummaging for another cigarette. She began to stroke him.

"Was?" he said.

"Yeah." She kept moving, keeping her eyes on his nearly hairless belly.

"Mine?" he said. She pressed her face against his knee.

Beauty leaned back, chair creaking, the only other sound skin against skin. She waited.

"Well?" His voice, so smooth, spiced. It could get her drunk, had got her drunk so many times. She remembered the first time he kissed her and how much she hated him then, how much she wanted to kill him. But nobody could kill Beauty. Nobody.

"What do you think?" she whispered against his knee. She was surprised it hurt. It was the type of question she was used to. It wasn't just Beauty asking things like that. Everybody did.

Beauty was back in the darkness, back behind the red dot of his cigarette, leaving her on the floor of the hotel with his prick between her fingers. "What happened to it?"

She changed hands and felt tears or sweat running between her breasts. She wished she hadn't asked him that question. Or at least, that he hadn't answered.

"Did you kill it?" he said all the way back behind his cigarette.

"No." She hadn't had time. She didn't even know before she started puking, started with a fever. They tested her at the clinic, taking blood and pictures of the dead thing inside of her. They cleaned what was left out and shot her full of antibiotics and said it was a common thing to happen. Especially to girls as young as she. Beauty let her work, let her kneel there and she didn't love him tonight. Didn't love him at all.

"I would have killed it," he said to her after he had stood and she was sticky with him. "I would have killed it," he said as he closed the bathroom door and left her there.

She held herself in the light from the window, her feet beneath her and the smell of smoke and Beauty everywhere. She put her slick hands against her belly, moving slowly from side to side.

"Twenty one," she said to the dark place Beauty had left behind.

***

When he left she lay on the bed. There was a hundred dollars on the night stand next to his empty pack of cigarettes. Beauty never left money before. Was it for the doctor? Or was it to make her feel like a whore? She stood in the shower with her hands on her belly. She didn't want to go home.

The streets were empty and her dress was wrinkled. Beauty liked dresses. It was his favorite, the red one she'd spent so much money on.

"It looks like sin," her mother had said when she saw it. They fought over it. Her mother and her. They fought over school, clothes, everything. Except Beauty. Her mother knew; she knew what Beauty did to her in that hotel room but she said nothing. The first night, after she walked home, her mother was waiting. They sat in the kitchen and her mother prayed. It was the same now, every time. She would open the door and her mother would be there, no matter how late. Her mother would take her hand and pray in that old woman's voice, in her old woman's language.

She stood on a corner, her high heels in her hand. The straps hurt her feet. They were for Beauty anyway. For him to take off of her. A car disappeared between streetlights, reappearing in those empty puddles of yellow. Her hair was wet from the shower and her makeup was long gone. Beauty's hundred dollars was heavy in her purse. Maybe she was a whore. Beauty's whore.

The car slowed down, a window burred open. A man inside, his face lit by the dashboard.

"Where you going?" the man said. She kept walking, her bare feet against the cold sidewalk.

"Do you need help?" he asked and she looked at him.

"I'm not a whore," she said.

"What?" the man leaned out his window, he smiled.

"I'm not a whore." She stopped walking, her shoes dangling from her crossed arms.

"Yeah, okay. Wanna ride?" the man glanced down the street.

"Leave," she said.

"Hey, don't be that way. I was just..."

"I'm not a whore!" she screamed and threw her shoes at the car, at the man, at something. The driver sped away, the car peek-a-booing its way through the streetlights.

She stood, shoeless, hair in her face.

"I'm not."

About the Author:

Cody T Luff's stories have recently appeared in *Menda City Review*, *Swamp Biscuits and Tea*, and *Paper Tape*, among others. He has an MFA in Creative Writing from Goddard College, and teaches in Portland, Oregon.

FLASH FICTION

A Man of God
Karina Bush

It was a slow evening. Nobody wanted me. Nobody nice anyway.

Two stoned videogamers with limps. No thank you. Me no no you speak.

Scruffy surfer Ozzie dude. Ok. Liked the girl next door. Fuck you.

Face like a diabetic's foot. Christ. No thank you.

Zaman. A big fat man. Ok. I like big fat men because I feel skinny with them but my legs always hurt after. I don't respect them though. I'd sucked him off before so at least I knew I'd be getting a tiny finger dick. A man of God, a business man, a family man. His crap suit smelt of his wife's cooking.

I saw his wife one day, walking behind him, he was moving through his prayer beads and he looked at me. She was stooped, her back nearly broken by hard work, and she looked at me too, like she knew. I'd know too if I was her.

He wanted everything and I wanted the money. No discount cunt. No kissing either, not that wet vascular face, I'd puke in the mouth.

I washed his penis and ran my tongue up it. His bowels rumbled. He licked me like the glutton he was, slurping, grunting, gulping at his tongue, big noisy pig crunching on bones, face resetting, big pig on a mission, big pig man twitching in the sty.

The smell of his wife's cooking was fucking rotten on his breath and his skin. I was glad to turn over. He did the homosexual act to me and he wanted me to do the homosexual act to him with my finger but my arm wasn't long enough to reach back. He was babbling. Then he said 'say I have a big cock', so I said it God, I said it.

He wept with his cum. Struggled to get his trousers up over his sweaty legs. Hilarious. Depressing bastard babbled on to the door. The room smelt of his wife's cooking all night and so did my hair.

Worthless fuck spat at my window one day after that. Fucking nutcase. Medieval scum. I almost paid a man to break his fat cunting pig arms.

About the Author:

Karina is an Irish poet and artist. For more visit karinabush.com. Karina has some poems published as part of the 48th Street Press broadside series. Free broadsides can be ordered on her website.

Anything Can Grow
Marion de Booy Wentzien

My brother Ronnie loved water. He'd untangle the green hose, connect it to the spigot and squirt the dirt in our barren backyard faithfully until bits of green grew. We lived on the outskirts of Tucson in the early seventies where our mother and stepfather ran a riding stable of bony, old horses.

Two nearby guest ranches used these horses for daily breakfast rides and for the weekly authentic barbecue that had square dancing on a concrete slab under cottonwoods alongside a wash. My uncle played fiddle while a cousin picked a banjo and occasionally yelled, "Yee-ha!"

While Mom dished up a wilted iceberg and radish salad, my stepfather grilled hotdogs. I served the "cowboy beans." I knew mom used regular canned baked beans and added Tabasco sauce along with a sprinkle of cinnamon. As usual Ronnie did nothing. He just rode around in circles on his dirt bike.

By the time he was ten, my brother was building aqueducts and filling them with the hose. Our yard was covered with whole towns of little mud huts with torn off bits of cactus, oleander and mesquite as trees. He even had a town square with a church of small animal bones. His creations from dirt, shrubs and bones were amazing even to me as a cynical twelve-year-old. He used to charge kids from school five cents to see what he'd created.

"That kid's going to be a great architect. Ronnie is going to change the world," Mom said. Ronnie would stand before his mud city, his skinny, tanned arms twisted together behind his back, rocking back on his dirty bare feet and smile, his green eyes dreamy.

I knew that he never washed behind his ears and that he kept a pet rat in our shared closet. My heart also knew that our mother loved him more than she loved me. I was rangy, freckle-faced, with tightly curled orange hair.

While I had the same green eyes Ronnie did, mine saw too much and got me into trouble.

"You and your smart mouth," Mom would say. You'd have thought I'd learn to duck, but the slap always caught me from cheek to chin.

*

Ronnie didn't become an architect. He robbed convenience stores. At nineteen he was shot dead.

I'm a psychiatrist.

About the Author:

Marion de Booy Wentzien received the PEN Fiction Award, twice, New Letters Award. Her stories have appeared in Seventeen, The San Francisco Chronicle, Scholastic Books, Story, On the Page, Big Ugly Review, The Quotable, Prime Number, Sonora Review, Bareback Lit, Red Fez, Cossack Review, Citron Review, Extract(s), Drafthorse, Solstice, ROAR, Spry and other literary journals. Amazon has her novel, Desert Shadows. She lives in Saratoga, CA with her husband and some rescued animals.

Moloff
Bob Sharp

Moloff. I have an image of him sitting in the kitchen of his two room shack, his belly hanging out. He opens his mouth to yawn and comes out with a friendly belch. He stretches, his hairy armpits open to the world. The bare light bulb dangling from the ceiling reflects on his bald and sweaty head. You don't want to look at an open light like that, I'm thinking. It sears your eyes. Everywhere you look you see the light bulb burning.

"Vengeance is sweet, vengeance is sweet." He was telling me about a fight he'd been in from his air force days. "It started in a bar. You know how it is. Another Air Force guy. He had his pals. I had mine. A challenge. Settle it like men. We went out in the street. I was stronger than him. I was sure I could take him. But it didn't go like that. He could box. He chopped me up and left me on the pavement like a piece of dog shit. My pals helped me up, but I knew even then it wouldn't be the same after... They didn't want to hang around so much and they always seemed down. I couldn't get over it. I wanted that fucker. I was stronger than him and I wanted him. So I went to the gym on the air base and signed up for boxing."

"The place was run by a weedy old guy. You'd see him out on the parade square with the ass of his shirt hanging out. You wouldn't think a guy like him would get anywhere in the service. After thirty years he was a sergeant. But he was a general in the gym. He didn't box much, but when I first went in he did a couple rounds with me. Couldn't lay a glove on him. He had to stop. He was gasping. After that he put me in with someone younger and told me what I was doing wrong. I went every day, week after week. Sometimes he'd climb into the ring and stop the session and give me or the other guy a pointer or two."

"After about four months of this I saw the guy I wanted in a night club. I invited him outside for a friendly waltz. He'd had too much to drink. I didn't want him like that but he was stupid. He thought it would be the same thing all over again. He came at me and I got him a good one. Put him on his ass. He got up. He was sober now, but it was too late. He couldn't do nothing. He'd come for me, I'd pop him on the kisser and he'd go down. On one knee. Or over on his side... Or on his back. I must've put him on his ass a dozen times. At last his buddies carried him away. It was alright--"

He grinned. Then his grin melted away. His ugly puss was getting sadder and sadder. He was old now. He'd been through the war without a scratch, but now he was old. Gone to flab. And he drank too much. And his pals were all gone. I knew he'd be getting into it now. I said I had to go. He sat and glumly watched the light swinging back and forth as I pulled on my jacket...

About the Author:

RAS is a retired clerk living in Toronto. He has worked at various jobs in the past 40 years and for a time swept the floors at the Bush Theatre in London. He grew up in Ottawa, Ontario.

The Immortal
Jackson Kinder

The end of the world has come and gone thousands of times. To each his own.

There was once a channel on TV, laconically entitled BYE, that brought the blank expressions of the sick and tired directly to the air conditioned living rooms of our houses and apartments, ostensibly in the noble pursuit of memorialization. The production quality was fantastic: dramatic golden lighting lent a heavenly aura to otherwise sterile hospitals, and refined Classical symphonies, when juxtaposed with the labored breaths of ghostly cancer patients and drug addicts, provided an understated, elegant soundtrack to mortality.

The immortal never watched. The channel was avoided with silent, cheery resoluteness by all; this wasn't a denial of its existence so much as a denial of one's own unpleasant preoccupation - no, dreadful, lurking fascination - with their own end.

"It's not really my style," mothers would confess to each other at book clubs, looking downward and wondering, astonished, how the topic had even been brought up. It was too honest for romantics, too obvious for nihilists. Even adolescent boys and sociopathic adults - the usual purveyors of the morbid, eerie - wholly avoided the channel at all costs. It was as if some invisible, spiritual force physically barred human consumption. No one could assuage their unacknowledged itch.

For the immortal to do anything besides sheepishly "accept" their fate (acceptance being a blatant charade) was mutinous. It was impossible to live or love without fully realizing the implications of one's immortality, yet it was equally impossible not to die while doing this. *True acceptance came at the end.* And so the enlightened remained isolated from the well, dying with their secrets.

One day, the channel inexplicably disappeared. Most everyone noticed its absence; a man looking for the Sunday football game, a child making his way to a beloved cartoon. In its place was substituted a 24 hour tennis network.

The collective reaction to this was the same as it had always been... meek, muted, almost paralyzed...it was like tossing a pebble into the ocean. There were a few brief segments regarding its disappearance on the nightly news, and a handful of discussions around dinner tables or through the hallways at work. Unanswerable questions arose endlessly like benign tumors - Who were the camera crew? Which hospitals were used for the show? Where did the funding come from, seeing that there were no advertisements? - yet they were murmured in such hushed, inoffensive tones that they evaporated instantaneously upon leaving ones mouth. The public didn't even go through their sentimental ritual of formulating conspiracy theories, a popular practice reserved for deceased pop stars and moon landings. It was a way of finding closure, but closure wasn't sought...a wave of collective apathy protected the masses.

This was how it disappeared, with or without consequence, leaving virtually no trace. The wind continued to blow listlessly through the trees, prized belongings mutated into meaningless artifacts. Dogs and men both howled implicitly at their respective masters. Warlords fathered children. As in before, the destructively visceral beauty and suffering of the human experience remained unfelt by all for the majority of their lives. Life was instead communicated in flashes and pangs, occasionally escaping from within its own packaging: a thick and translucent plastic wrap. WARNING! It screamed. DO NOT TOUCH.

The beautiful lighting and Classical soundtracks were gone. Of course, the dying continued to die. An infinite amount of personal apocalypse came and went in any given moment. The brief period for which the channel had mysteriously broadcast their epilogues obviously hadn't had any effects on the merciless passing of time. In the end, there was neither cold finality nor epic rebirth - a wispy of tendril of smoke danced tentatively off the warmth of a dying ember, and the immortal bid farewell.

About the Author:

Jackson Kinder is a recording engineer and producer from Berkeley, CA. He is currently crafting an album with his band, The New Soul Era, due out by the end of 2014. In his free time, he enjoys knitting and croquet. He is inspired by the works of Faulkner, Georges Perec, and Junot Diaz.

FEATURED POET

MICHAEL E. STONE was born in England in 1938. His family moved to Australia in 1941, where he received his schooling, up to the completion of his BA (Hons.) degree in 1960. He lives in Jerusalem with his family. He has published poems in numerous literary journals and e-zines as well as translations of medieval Armenian poetry. His poetry has also been anthologized in a number of collections. A book of his work, *Selected Poems*, was published by Cyclamens and Swords Press in 2010. A poetic translation of *Adamgirk'*, a medieval Armenian epic about Adam and Eve in 6,000 lines, appeared with Oxford University Press in 2007. Some of his poems have been translated into Armenian.

Stone's academic activities have been devoted to two different disciplines, Jewish literature and thought in the period of the Second Temple, including the Dead Sea Scrolls, and Armenian Studies. His research and academic publications have been divided between these two fields. He holds the degrees of PhD (Harvard) and DLitt. (Melbourne). He was appointed to the Hebrew University of Jerusalem in 1966 and became Gail Levin de Nur Professor of Religious Studies and Professor of Armenian Studies in 1980. He is now retired. He holds an Honorary DHL (Hebrew Union College), Honorary Doctor (Armenian National Academy of Sciences). He is recipient of the Landau Prize for Contribution to the Humanities (Israel).

My poetry emerges, I believe, from the pattern of tensions with which I live. It holds the very differing dimensions of myself and my life experience in a balance. So the diverse cultures in which I live and have lived – Australia and Israel – produce rich perceptions, those of the insider-outsider looking at both. My intense preoccupation with another linguistic and cultural tradition, the Armenian, provides yet a third, quite different dimension and a third cultural and literary language. Yet another flavour! The difference between the way I use my mind as a trained scholar and the accessing of the subjective dimension of being that poetry demands is another great tension. Wyndham Lewis puts poetry outside the realm of "the mind-that-sweats" –very true, but a struggle nevertheless. I am 75 years old, and I also live between the now I experience daily and the past I remember, between the habits and values of a lifetime and the mores of this generation. I live in a country with a long history, a wise friend once said "too much history", and in an unsettled part of the world. Here too is a stimulating, creative and sometimes discordant discourse between different aspects of time and place and peoples. The sparks of poetry beaten on this anvil help sustain my life's coherence.

Action on screen
Michael E. Stone

CPU alive with
binary silicone switches.
switches, on / off,
choices.

On and off
life and death.

Life's river flows,
death stops it

and you cannot twice step
into that same river.

Life flows on a bed of
      sand, silicone,
         binary choices.

And a pike sits under the ledge
      ready to snap it up.

November 5, 2012

Apprentices
Michael E. Stone

When she teaches her students,
does she seek their growth
or her own immortality?

Does she project her mind's light
onto reflecting mind-mirrors?
Does her pride make her declaim
her greater garner of details?

Yes, there's some truth in that,
some but not all. For mind's
mirror reflects back,
changed and refocused
fresh insights transmitted
from new minds and to them.

The looking glass shows
a familiar used face, but
mind's ever new sight
views its own perspective.

So, teaching is
more how than what,
two-fold,
a giving, a taking,
a sending, receiving.

Humbling.

Changing lenses
Michael E. Stone

They change the eye's lens when
it loses focus, blurs.

Now does the world really have
such sharp edges?
Maybe the blur was closer
to the truth.

October 2010

Matter over Mind
Michael E. Stone

in a dusty room
at 3 pm,
a bright young scholar
lectures,

so intensely!

in the audience
everyone over fifty
(and some under)
nods off,
shudders awake,
and nods off again.

Idiocy
Michael E. Stone

idiocy, idiocy in the short time
between conception's passion
and death's cessation

inevitable idiocy towards
life's levels of being
parents and past and poets
who begat us in body and in spirit

and love not being selves,
hate selves but not others
or selves instead of others

or for some, those who kill,
others instead of selves,

to kill to hate themselves.
as the others,
self's parts.

instead of joy, love, life.

December 2008

It's Gone
Michael E. Stone

It's gone, the fishing village,
wrapped around the bay,
with a lighthouse,
and small, dirty, working boats,
nets, and fish merchants.

Now it has upmarket restaurants,
a fair with colored tents
where they hawk
organic stuff,
Lebanese food,
baklava, fossil fish,
and Guiness T-shirts.

By the breakwater
half-tame seals beg
for crusts of bread.

Each time I've been back,
it grew more so, till
at lunch today,
in a fake-old pub,
with fake evening gloom,
fake fire burned in the grate.

I cannot go there again,
the village I used to visit
is gone.

Dublin
July 18, 2012

Featured Artist

CHRIS CASTLE is native of Toronto, Ontario. She is an artist and a midwife. She most often works in oils but has recently begun a series of pen and ink drawings. Her idea is to breakdown complex ideas and ideologies into their simplest, purist, most basic form. She tries to see the world as if she was a child and relate her visions in the same way a child would. "Art doesn't have to be complicated. It doesn't even have to be pretty, it just has to be done."

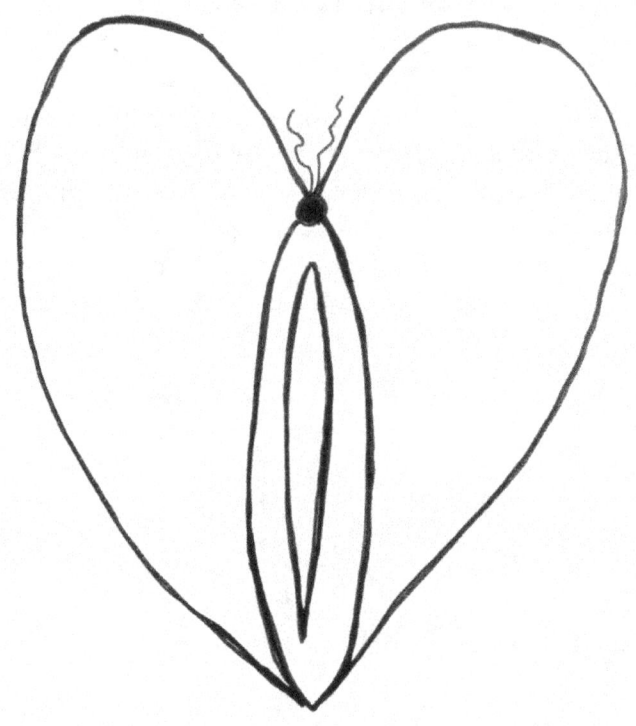

"A Butterfly?"
8 x12
Ink on paper
2014

$$100 + 100 = 100,100$$

"Positive Thinking"
8 x 12
Ink on paper
2014

●

"Atheism"
8 x 12
Ink on paper
2014

"Monotheism"
8 x 12
Ink on paper
2014

"Polytheism"
8 x 12
Ink on paper
2014

THOUGHT

About Attraction:

Beauty is not what we see, it is what we feel. At the basest level, once all superficialities are stripped away, something is beautiful not because of the way the eyes perceive it, but for the way the heart feels it.

~ T. Fenson